Pickering Castle
NORTH YORKSHIRE

LAWRENCE BUTLER MA, PhD, FSA, MIFA

The grassy mound and the curtain walls punctuated by tall towers are the most prominent features of this royal fortress. The mound was raised by William the Conqueror. The stonework on the mound and around the inner courtyard or ward is of early thirteenth-century date and was built for Henry III when this castle was a necessary defence against the Scots. The outer entrance, the curtain wall and its three towers were built on the orders of Edward II in 1323–6. These were the last additions to the defences. Later improvements concerned the New Hall and the Constable's Lodging, reflecting the castle's role as a centre for hunting in the Forest of Pickering and for the administration of its local territory. By the time of the Civil War its military purpose had long been abandoned and most of the castle was in decay.

This guidebook contains a quick tour (centre pages), a description of the buildings, and a history of the castle and its changing role.

Contents

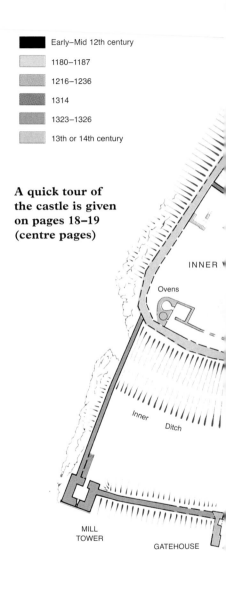

Early–Mid 12th century

1180–1187

1216–1236

1314

1323–1326

13th or 14th century

A quick tour of the castle is given on pages 18–19 (centre pages)

INNER W

Ovens

Inner Ditch

MILL TOWER

GATEHOUSE

0   10   20   30

Metres

Published by English Heritage,
1 Waterhouse Square, 138-142 Holborn, London EC1N 2ST
Copyright © English Heritage 1993
First published by English Heritage 1993
Reprinted 1997, 1999, 2001, 2003, 2005, 2008, 2015
Revised reprint 2012; 2013

Photographs by English Heritage Photography Section
and copyright of English Heritage unless otherwise stated

Visit our website at www.english-heritage.org.uk

Printed in England by Pureprint Group
C65 03/15 04150
ISBN 978 1 85074 434 4

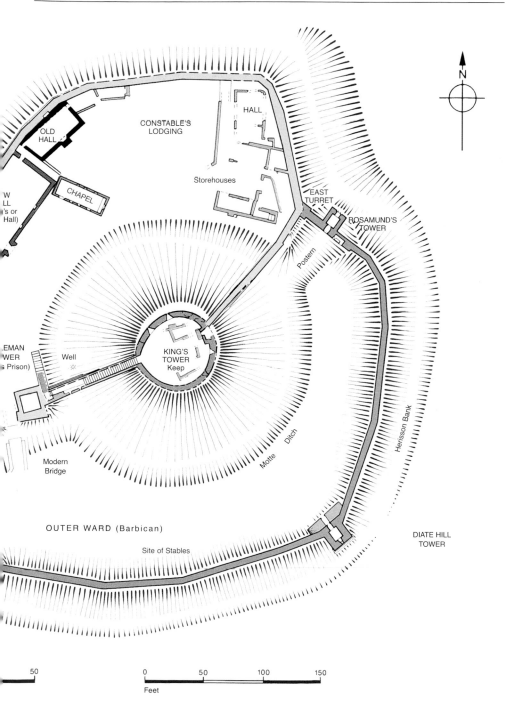

N

CONSTABLE'S
LODGING

HALL

OLD
HALL

W
LL
's or
Hall)

CHAPEL

Storehouses

EAST
TURRET

ROSAMUND'S
TOWER

Postern

EMAN
WER
s Prison)

Well

KING'S
TOWER
Keep

Herisson Bank

Motte   Ditch

Modern
Bridge

OUTER WARD (Barbican)

DIATE HILL
TOWER

Site of Stables

50

0   50   100   150

Feet

Tour of the Castle

The castle is dominated by the stone keep on its earthen mound

Standing on the edge of the North Yorkshire moors, with extensive views over the surrounding countryside, Pickering Castle is a fine example of motte-and-bailey design. It was started by William the Conqueror shortly after the Norman Conquest as part of a successful attempt to gain control over the North. The later stone castle is well preserved, with many of its towers standing nearly to their full height. For most of its active life the castle's role was to provide fine accommodation for the king and his retinue when he visited the northern counties. In the king's absence the castle served as a local power-base, where royal authority was represented by the sheriff. Through the law courts which operated from the castle, hunting and other rights in the nearby forest were controlled; these courts continued to function long after the castle's defensive role had ended.

The keep

The tour starts at the heart of the castle's defences, the keep. From the outer courtyard or ward, walk across the bridge leading to the inner ward and, turning right, climb to the top of the stone steps.

The grassy mound up which the stairway climbs is a man-made hill or 'motte', built on William the Conqueror's orders to command the surrounding territory. From this vantage point it would have been possible to look southwards across the Vale of Pickering towards Malton, to control the valley edge road

from Scarborough on the east coast to
Helmsley and Ryedale on the west, and to
dominate the track leading northwards
over the moors to Whitby. The earth
mound topped by a timber tower would
have given a psychological as well as a
physical advantage to the soldiers
stationed on its summit. Their leader
could easily command all parts of the
castle defences simultaneously. Today the
motte and ditches are left to grow wild for
three-year periods, before being cut back.
The result is a great variety of flora and
fauna, including rare plants, owls and bats.

From the motte summit can be seen the
two main divisions of the castle: north-west
towards Newton Dale is the inner ward,
with its closely packed domestic buildings
set on the edge of the rocky valley; south-
east towards the town is the outer ward,
enclosed by a curtain wall which sheltered
the garrison store-sheds and stables.

The timber tower was set within a
circular palisade or fence, later rebuilt in
stone to form a 'shell' keep, parts of which
survive. This outer wall, itself possibly a
rebuilding of an earlier stone enclosure,
dates to the early part of Henry III's reign
(1216–72). A ring of lean-to buildings in
the inner area would have provided a
secure private lodging for the king; some of
their foundations are still visible. In
Edward II's reign (1307–27) the keep was
known as the King's Tower, but by Tudor
times it was in ruin.

The wall of the shell keep is roughly
circular inside but is made up of short
lengths of straight walling on the outside.
This outside face uses squarish rubble
blocks with smooth ashlar dressings at the
base, at the quoins (forming the junctions of
the straight lengths) and around the window
slits. The two full-height splayed arrow-slits
on the north side are all that survive of a
series of windows, probably ten, that were
originally evenly spaced around the tower.
The flat part of the wall above them shows
the original height of the wall-walk.

This reconstruction painting shows how the first wooden castle may have appeared in the early twelfth century (painting: Ivan Lapper)

Faceted exterior wall of the keep

The shell keep originally had two entrances, both giving access to the tops of the walls which ran up the slopes of the mound. The lesser entrance was on the east and the steps leading up from inside the keep to its doorway are still visible.

This entrance would have given patrolling soldiers access to a continuous wall-walk around the inner ward. The major entrance was on the west but its archway has been destroyed.

Now descend from the mound to the point where the steps turn at a right angle. The steps run along the wall-walk at the same level as in medieval times; on the right there may have been a low stone wall. On the left a screen wall is pierced with arrow-slits, probably added to the wall-top in John's reign (1199–1216). A later heightening made the southern (left-hand) wall thicker and provided a higher parapet walk; one arrow-slit of the earlier work was then blocked.

Inner ward

From the angle of the steps look down at the inner ward. The motte and inner ward are the oldest parts of the castle; indeed they were originally the whole of the castle. The outer ward was added later, first protected by an earthen bank and ditch, and then, in the fourteenth century,

The Coleman Tower (left) and screen wall protecting the approach to the keep

by a stone wall. Exactly the same sequence happened earlier with the inner ward. First, in the late eleventh century, it was defended by a timber wall with a deep ditch outside it on the south and east. Then the timbers were replaced by stone during the late twelfth century.

This courtyard formed the domestic heart of the castle: it contained the main hall, private rooms, kitchens, food stores and brewhouse. When the king was in residence it would have been teeming with life and activity. When he was absent the main resident would have been the constable or steward, who had his own private apartments and was in command of a small permanent garrison. At such times the hall would have been used as a law court with the chaplain probably acting as the clerk of the court. The inner ward was at first defended by a timber fence, but this was replaced in stone during the late twelfth century.

Coleman Tower

At the angle of the steps it is possible to look into the interior of the Coleman Tower. The lower part of this plain square tower was probably the work of Henry II (1154–89) or one of his sons and was built to control the adjacent entrance to the inner ward. The ground-floor level was probably used as a prison: this function is mentioned in a document of 1323, and, as was usual in medieval prisons, there are no openings for windows or doors. Offenders against the forest laws and petty criminals, thieves and brigands from the Pickering district would have been locked up here. The prison was later moved to the Mill Tower in the outer ward.

The upper floor would have housed the soldiers defending the staircase and guarding the entrance. One doorway led to the staircase, another (now blocked) to a room over the entrance passage, where the drawbridge and portcullis mechanism

The Castle well

could be worked. The tower roof could also be reached from here. On the north side of this floor a small square-headed window survives, but there were probably also arrow-slits on the south side, overlooking the bridge and ditch.

The tower is of rubble, faced with ashlar quoins and plinth. The upper floor was repaired in 1323–26; at the same time a parapet was erected on top of the tower, resting on a moulded cornice, and the lead on the roof was recast.

The Coleman Tower probably takes its name from a constable or honorary porter who occasionally occupied it; it is known by this name in all the surveys of the castle carried out during the Tudor period.

At the bottom of the steps is the castle well at the foot of the ditch on the right. It was dug through the limestone early in the castle's history. During Edward II's reign a cord was purchased for the well bucket: it measured 20 ells (75ft or 23m long), indicating the depth of the well.

Looking back from here at the steps you can see that it rests on top of a fine piece of walling spanning the ditch surrounding the mound (the motte ditch). This and the corresponding wall on the other side of the mound date from Henry II's time and replaced the earlier timber palisade.

In this reconstruction painting, the entrance can be seen to the left of the Coleman Tower (painting: Ivan Lapper)

Entrance

The Coleman Tower flanks what was originally the main entrance to the castle, before the curtain wall and towers of the outer ward were added. Later it became the entrance to the inner ward. It was protected by a gateway, now completely vanished, and by the inner ditch which still survives. The ditch was spanned by a succession of timber bridges, of which the present modern bridge is the latest. The first recorded bridge was repaired in 1185–6 and further repairs were ordered in 1238. A moveable bridge was replaced by a drawbridge in 1323 on the orders of Edward II. The drawbridge would have been pulled up against a pair of wooden gates and the arch of the stone entrance passage. This passage stood forward of the line of the curtain wall and its foundations survive alongside and below the present bridge.

Above the passage was a store-room which in Tudor times was used to house the rolls and records of the manor and the forest. In a survey of 1537 it was known as the Grayss Chamber (perhaps meaning His Grace's Chamber – the king was referred to as 'His Grace') but it was not in domestic use. By 1621 it was completely decayed.

Courtyard

Keeping the curtain wall on your left-hand side, you can see the foundations of the domestic buildings which filled the inner ward between the entrance and the New Hall.

A narrow range of buildings was set against the curtain wall; the thin foundations suggest a half-timbered structure. At the western end beyond a square room are two circular stone ovens, their base stones much reddened by fire. This range probably represents a brewhouse and a bakehouse.

The west curtain wall overlooking the Pickering Beck is largely destroyed but there are further foundations visible in the grass. These are likely to be the kitchens, larder and pantry serving the New Hall. The financial accounts of Edward II show that there was also a latrine here, probably situated high in the curtain wall and discharging down the hillside.

A fourteenth-century kitchen scene, from the Luttrell Psalter (British Library)

Chapel

The chapel is the only surviving roofed building. The first mention of a chapel is in 1227 when a chalice and two vestments were ordered for it. It is therefore probable that the chapel building was started in 1226–7. A chaplain was appointed in 1238 supported by royal income. Pickering Castle had a resident chaplain from that date until 1547, when all chantry chapels were closed and their income confiscated under Henry VIII. The chaplain's income came from two main sources. In 1374 John of Gaunt, Duke of Lancaster, granted the chaplain the revenues of the Hospital of St Nicholas outside the castle on condition that he maintained its fabric. Soon after 1460 Edward IV established a chantry of Our Lady within the castle, giving the chaplain additional income. Money would be given in return for masses sung for the souls of the dead. By 1546, however, the castle chapel was known as the Chapel of St Nicholas and was used for saying masses for the souls of the Dukes of Lancaster. A century later the chapel was being used as a court-room and no longer had a religious function.

The original stonework of the chapel is of small rubble. The four western lancet windows, two on either side, are original, as is the doorway with a pointed head and outer dripstone. The chapel had seven windows which were newly glazed in 1325. The west end has been partly shortened and the east end shows a variety of changes, the large ashlar blocks marking later work dating from the Tudor period. The chapel was much restored early in the nineteenth century and reroofed again about forty years ago. The interior now contains an exhibition on the castle and its role as a hunting lodge.

New Hall

To your right as you leave the chapel are the foundations of a spacious building. The New Hall was rebuilt in 1314 for the Countess Alice (de Lacy), wife of Thomas, Earl of Lancaster. It cost £341 15s 8d (more than £35,000 in modern money) and had two storeys and a stone-tiled roof. The private chamber of the countess may well have occupied the upper floor at the northern end. This was an elaborately plastered room with a fireplace decorated with plaster of Paris. Four hundred cartloads of stone were used to build the New Hall, although it was predominantly timber-framed. In 1621 John Norden, a land surveyor employed by James I, described it as of 'post and pan' construction, meaning of timber posts and infilled panels of plaster-covered wattlework. Much of the surviving architectural detail belongs to the late twelfth and early thirteenth centuries; it must therefore be assumed that the new work concentrated on the upper storey and the roof, perhaps also providing larger windows.

The Tudor surveys call this building the King's Hall or the Mote (Meeting) Hall, and by then it was in regular use as a court-house. However, the upper floor and roof timbers were in decay and by Norden's time it was unsafe to use. Thirty years later in 1651 it had been abandoned and 'was almost fallen to the ground'.

The chapel from the north

Reconstruction of the New Hall in use as a court-room. The presidential chair is on the right (painting: Ivan Lapper)

At the south-east corner is the principal doorway, the bases of its triple jamb shafts showing that they supported a finely moulded arch. Two steps lead down into the hall and on the left the south wall contains doorways to the pantry and buttery. On the right the east wall has two window recesses. On the west, in the curtain wall, are two further recesses; the southerly one is mostly destroyed but it appears to have housed a fireplace. The

Norman chevron moulding in the New Hall

northerly one was framed within an arch, of which the left-hand jamb shaft base survives; within the arch was a stone seat. There was a similar recessed seat in the Old Hall (see below) and both may have served as the presidential chair of the lord's steward when the halls were used for law courts. The hall is over 40ft (13m) wide and its roof would have been supported on two rows of wooden pillars.

At the north-west corner of the New Hall a doorway leads into a passage or gallery between the two halls. This passage allowed the countess to have private access to the chapel through a west doorway (now blocked); in 1314 it was ordered that the passage be roofed with planks.

Old Hall
Close to the curtain wall a doorway leads into the Old Hall. This is the earliest

Decorated Norman arch in the Old Hall (drawing: Kate Wilson)

surviving stone structure in the castle. When it was built the curtain wall was still a timber palisade. Evidence that the hall was initially free-standing can be seen in the exposed foundation of the original west wall. Later, probably at the end of the twelfth century, when the curtain wall was rebuilt in stone, the west wall was pulled down and the hall slightly enlarged to the width permitted by the new curtain wall. A prominent feature in the new west wall is the moulded and decorated Norman arch which framed the seat recess (mentioned earlier). Nearly opposite the seat was the fireplace, indicated by a projection on the east wall to support the chimney. The slightness of the wall foundations suggests that this hall also had timber-framed walls.

After the construction of the New Hall the Old Hall would have continued in use as guest chambers or as a servants' hall. Two small rectangular buildings beyond the north-east doorway of this hall are presumably domestic rooms of twelfth-century or later date.

Constable's Lodging

In the north-east corner of the inner ward are the low stone foundations of a group of half-timbered buildings. None of the stone foundations aligns with any part of the stone curtain wall, suggesting that earlier timber structures were gradually replaced in stone. The 'Constable's Place' is named in the duchy accounts for 1441–3, but the complex is best described in the 1537 survey:

> And from the ... chapel by the space of 40 yd [37m] stands an old house called the Constable Lodging having in the same a hall of length 10 yd [9m], in breadth 7 yd [6.4m] and two cross chambers with buttery, pantry, cellar and kitchen covered with slate, and two old houses of office for rude and other stuff, and two chambers on them, all of which be in decay of timber by estimation 40 ton.

The buildings were not mentioned in the survey of 1621 but by 1651 it was reported that 'on the backside of [the inner ward] lyeth a third Court ... in which hath been diverse buildings but now ruined and fallen to the ground'.

It is still possible to identify the hall and its ancillary buildings and, across a small court, the two store-rooms or 'houses of office'. The odd wall angles are caused by lean-to structures having been set against the curtain wall. The whole complex was made more private by being hidden behind a narrow western wall; at its northern end stood an earlier flight of steps that once led up to the wall-walk.

The constable was originally the military commander of the garrison and was responsible for guarding the castle for the king at all times; his lodgings would have been near the castle's main entrance. The steward was responsible for the

The Constable's Lodging seen from the keep. The rooms in the foreground were probably store-rooms

Outer ward looking south-west towards the Mill Tower

smooth running of the estate and the administration of law and order; he presided over the courts and, if resident, would have had his lodging near the hall and private chambers. As the offices of constable, steward and bailiff became amalgamated the constable and his family would then have occupied a suite of rooms with a less defensive function. It would have been a lodging more suited to a member of the minor gentry than to a well-paid clerk. At Scarborough Castle the steward and constable John Mosdale erected a hall and lodgings during the period 1393–1443. The hall at Pickering is similar but smaller; it may have been built by David Roucliffe, steward and constable 1393–1407.

The composition of the curtain wall can be seen in cross-section in the south-eastern corner of this group of buildings. The wall had outer facings of carefully coursed rubble blocks and an inner core of very roughly laid stones. With such a construction technique there was always a danger that once water and root penetration reached into the core, the outer face would be forced outwards to bulge, crack and fall away. In 1537 it was noted that 30ft (9m) of the curtain wall of the inner ward had fallen down; this probably refers to the south-western side of the wall where there is now a large gap.

Before descending into the outer ward through a gap in the cross-wall near the motte ditch, notice on your right the fine stretch of wall spanning the ditch; the slight horizontal offsets on both inner and outer faces allow it to decrease in width as it climbs the motte slope.

Outer ward

Beyond the deep inner ditch lies the level ground of the outer ward. The terms outer and inner wards first appear in the financial accounts of the fifteenth century;

sometimes the keep was regarded as the innermost ward and the area containing the halls was known as the middle ward. The outer ward was formerly called the barbican because it shielded the castle proper, giving additional defence on the weaker sides near the town. There may have been some kind of defence here right from the very beginning. In the reign of John, when the outer ward is first recorded, it consisted of a bank and ditch. On top of the bank was a palisade of pointed stakes and on the outer bank slope was a herisson (literally a 'hedgehog') bristling with stakes. The wooden palisade was replaced by a stone curtain wall in 1323–6 on the orders of Edward II. The wall and its four towers were all built at the same time as part of the last major defensive upgrading of the castle. There was no similar upgrading of the inner ward which retained its older curtain wall without interval towers.

Rosamund's Tower

The northernmost of the new towers stands astride the inner ditch. This allowed a small gate or postern to be placed in the ditch bottom. Edward II's instructions of 1323 included the building of a postern next to the King's Tower (i.e. the keep) but it is not known why or when the name Rosamund was first associated with the building. Henry II's mistress was known as the 'Fair Rosamund', but she had died more than a century earlier. The tower is so named by the antiquary John Leland, describing his visit to Pickering in about 1535, and is referred to by this name in the Tudor and Stuart surveys.

In common with the other towers of the outer ward it projects beyond the outer curtain wall. It is constructed of larger, squarer rubble blocks than the earlier work and has ashlar dressings and a parapet supported by a moulded cornice. At the bottom of the tower is the postern

Rosamund's Tower. The remains of the east turret can be seen on the left

passage, which was closed by a small drawbridge towards the outer ditch. A single chain or rope for lowering the bridge passed through a hole which is still visible over the centre of the arch.

The ground floor is reached through a small chamfered and fluted round-headed doorway on the outer edge of the inner ditch; this leads into a wall passage lit by two small rectangular windows. The room itself is lit by a cruciform arrow-slit, and joist-holes show the position of the floor. The upper room of the tower (which is no longer accessible) was entered by steps from the curtain wall a little further east. A corridor with two narrow rectangular slits leads through the tower at this level and continues on through the added east turret (see below) to the wall-walk of the inner ward. This room was provided with a latrine in the thickness of the wall and with two windows of differing sizes. On the south face of the parapet is a small cruciform arrow-slit, set askew and more decorative than defensive.

Looking back from the outer ward towards the inner ward it is possible to see the east turret, which was added at the

The sallyport seen from outside the castle

junction of the two curtain walls in order to control access from the earlier wall-walk to the later one. Its fine ashlar plinth and quoins are characteristic of the 1323–6 work. It is one of two turrets mentioned in the 1537 survey; the other was probably at the corresponding junction of the two curtains at the south-west corner of the inner ward.

Between Rosamund's Tower and Diate Hill Tower is an impressive stretch of curtain wall. It is set out in short straight lengths with each angle accentuated and strengthened by a vertical line of ashlar blocks. It still stands to the height of the wall-walk but the external battlements have fallen.

Diate Hill Tower

The name of this tower first appears in the 1537 survey; in the surveys of 1621 and 1651 it is simply Dyet Tower. The name may derive from the Middle English 'diet' (a day's work) and perhaps refers to a feudal duty of so many days' work a year on the herisson and palisade before the stone wall was built. Certainly a similar duty called 'hirsons' continued to be levied in Pickering well into the nineteenth century, long after the necessity to repair the castle's outer wall had ceased.

The tower stands at an abrupt change of direction in the curtain wall. It is quite likely that the entire curtain wall was built first, in partly dressed rubble, and that the tower, faced with ashlar above the wall-walk, was added later. The tower is of three storeys and has a modern roof. Entry to the ground-floor and first-floor rooms is through plain chamfered doorways with round heads. The ground-floor room is lit by a single window opposite the entrance. The upper floors are not now accessible but their arrangements are visible from below and from the exterior of the castle. The

Diate Hill Tower

first-floor doorway was reached by a wide flight of steps built against the back of the tower and formerly carried on an arch across the approach to the room below. The main room was lit by two windows and was approached by a passage with a latrine in the wall thickness; a newel staircase led to the second floor, the western wall-walk and the roof.

The second-floor room is larger than those below owing to a reduction in the thickness of the walls. It is well lit by a two-light transomed window with cusped heads dating from the fifteenth century. On the west wall is a square-headed fireplace with moulded jambs and top, and a moulded mantel above. Beside it is a small square-headed window. In the north-east corner a door leads to a latrine, while in the east wall are two recessed cupboards and a small square-headed window. This made an attractive self-contained room for a captain of the guard or a person of similar rank.

Stables

Between the Diate Hill Tower and the gatehouse the curtain wall stands up to wall-walk height with the parapet surviving in places. Against this stretch of wall a slight flattening of the inner bank indicates the site of the stables. When hunting played a prominent part in the castle's daily life, stabling for horses,

kennels for hounds and rooms for their grooms and handlers would have been essential.

According to the Tudor surveys there was a stone-roofed two-storeyed building with three rooms on each floor, measuring 240ft (73m) long by 18ft (5.5m) broad and 18ft (5.5m) high. It was partly of stone, partly of wood, the upper storey presumably being timber-framed. This range is likely to have been of fifteenth-century date.

Mill Tower

This square tower, at the south-western corner of the outer ward, has usually been known as the Mill Tower. A mill near the castle is recorded from Henry III's time, perhaps referring to a water mill standing beside the Pickering Beck in the valley below. Cleaning the castle's mill-ponds and repairing its dam wall were regular labour services – similar to the repair of the herisson – for the bond tenants. Alternatively, it is possible that the tower took its name from a horse mill in this corner of the outer ward. This is suggested by a statement in the 1537 survey that by that time there was no longer a horse mill at the castle. A horse-powered crushing wheel would have been used for grinding coarse flour and animal feed. The tower itself was in disrepair in 1537, but had been put in good order by 1621. The ground floor was probably then used as a prison while the upper-floor chamber with its fireplace and latrine could have housed the gaoler. By 1651 the outer walls were still sound but the interior had been stripped of its lead, iron and timber and so could no longer be used as a prison.

Most of the Mill Tower projects beyond the curtain walls; on its western side the ground falls away steeply. It is built of partly dressed rubble with ashlar quoins and a moulded plinth; there is a

The Mill Tower from the outer ward

string-course at first-floor level and a hollow-chamfered cornice supports the parapet. The ground floor is entered from the outer ward through a double doorway linked by a short vaulted passage. The sockets for the hinges and latches show that the first door opened inwards and the second outwards, measures of security which suggest the tower may have been designed as a prison from the first. The lower room is lit only by a narrow slit. The first-floor room, which is larger, was entered through a similar double doorway from steps against the western side of the curtain wall. On the west in the thickness of the wall is a latrine discharging into the ditch. On the south was a large two-light square-headed window, the tracery of

A Quick Tour of Pickering Castle

1 Keep Large earth and stone mound of the Norman castle crowned by a later shell keep with lean-to buildings forming a ring of private rooms; known as the King's Tower *(page 4)*

2 Coleman Tower Two-storey tower of 1180–87, repaired a century later; contained a prison below and guard room above *(page 7)*

3 Entrance Two-storey building with an entrance passage below and a defended room above; later used as the records office *(page 8)*

4 Inner Ward Bailey or courtyard of the Norman castle, containing rooms for sleeping, eating and cooking to accommodate the king's household *(page 6)*

5 New Hall Fine fourteenth-century hall for feasting; also used as a court-room for the trial of forest offenders; known as the King's Hall or Mote Hall *(page 9)*

6 Chapel Small thirteenth-century chapel, served by a domestic chaplain until 1547. Later used as the court-room when the New Hall became unsafe to use *(page 9)*

7 Old Hall Earliest stone building in the castle, of early twelfth-century date. Used for feasting and as a court-room *(page 10)*

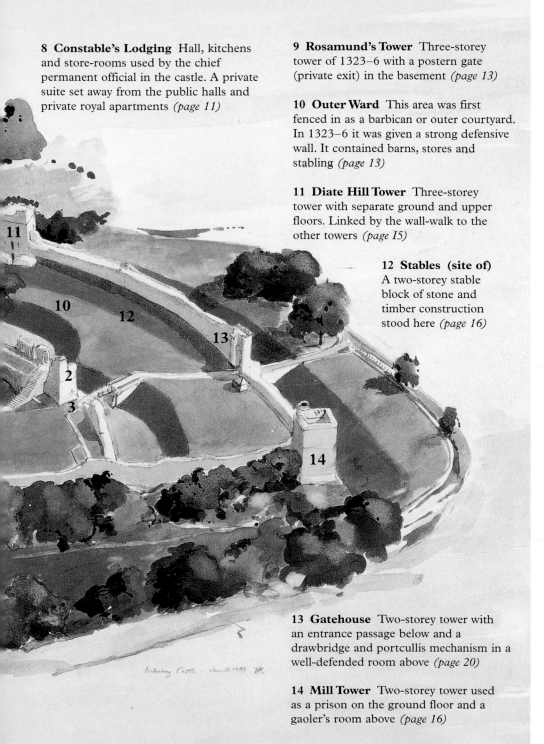

8 Constable's Lodging Hall, kitchens and store-rooms used by the chief permanent official in the castle. A private suite set away from the public halls and private royal apartments *(page 11)*

9 Rosamund's Tower Three-storey tower of 1323–6 with a postern gate (private exit) in the basement *(page 13)*

10 Outer Ward This area was first fenced in as a barbican or outer courtyard. In 1323–6 it was given a strong defensive wall. It contained barns, stores and stabling *(page 13)*

11 Diate Hill Tower Three-storey tower with separate ground and upper floors. Linked by the wall-walk to the other towers *(page 15)*

12 Stables (site of) A two-storey stable block of stone and timber construction stood here *(page 16)*

13 Gatehouse Two-storey tower with an entrance passage below and a drawbridge and portcullis mechanism in a well-defended room above *(page 20)*

14 Mill Tower Two-storey tower used as a prison on the ground floor and a gaoler's room above *(page 16)*

which has been broken away. On the east wall is a square-headed fireplace, and in the north-east corner a doorway leads to a short newel staircase contained in the circular turret, giving access to the tower roof.

The length of curtain wall between the Mill Tower and the gatehouse has survived almost to wall-walk height, but the stretch running north from the Mill Tower is ruinous, except near the tower, where the broken triangular top of the parapet can still be seen. However, where the curtain wall crosses the inner ditch it still stands to full height. At its junction with the corner of the older circuit of the inner ward there was presumably direct access from one wall-walk to the other; this would have been the position of the west turret, similar in form to the turret still visible north-west of Rosamund's Tower (p 15).

The gate passage at Pickering was probably similar to that of Walmgate Bar, York (photo: RCHM(E))

Gatehouse

When compared with the Lancastrian castles of Pontefract and Lancaster or the Percy castle of Warkworth, the gatehouse at Pickering is a modest and lightly defended opening. Nevertheless, it is likely that the gate passage was protected by a drawbridge and a double door set in an arched entrance, the shape of which can be made out in the stonework above the present opening. This entrance was flanked by wall-walks. These would have allowed the defenders to attack any intruders who had broken down the drawbridge but were halted in front of the wooden doors. A similar arrangement may be seen at Walmgate Bar in York. The order for the building of the gatehouse at Pickering was given in 1323 but it may not have been completed at the time of Edward II's death in 1327.

Exterior of the castle

A circuit of the exterior of the castle gives you an idea of how it must have appeared to intending attackers and allows you to appreciate the difficulty of making a direct assault on the walls. Leaving the castle over the gatehouse bridge, turn left, and walk round the castle in an anti-clockwise direction.

The stretch of wall between the gatehouse and Rosamund's Tower is the most impressive. Here the curtain wall stands to wall-walk height; only the battlemented or crenellated parapet is missing. The towers have plinths of sloping masonry and string-courses at first-floor level. The shoots for the latrines are a prominent feature. At the two points where the wall changes direction there are corbelled projections to allow the watchmen to overlook areas of concealed ground. The great depth of the outer ditch outside Rosamund's Tower shows how difficult it would have been for

A projecting timber hourd could be used to defend the castle walls (drawing from R Allen Brown, Castles: A History and Guide, *1980)*

attackers to approach the tower and how well protected the postern gate was.

Beyond Rosamund's Tower the footpath runs on a level platform below the earlier curtain wall of the inner ward. The hillside falls precipitously to the right, and would have provided valuable protection when it was clear of trees. Neither the platform nor the exposed rock-face are medieval, but are the result of later quarrying, some of it to obtain stone for the castle and the houses of the town, some of it to undermine and rob stone from the castle. At the north-east corner of the inner ward curtain wall a section still stands up to parapet level. It is possible to see three socket holes which may have held timber hourds or brattices supporting a protected wall-walk outside the stone wall; from this, the castle's defenders could have tried to prevent the wall-base from being undermined by picking or battering. Much of this older curtain wall has collapsed over the cliff-face but behind the two halls it is better preserved: the wall-face has been repaired and provided with a plinth, probably in the decade 1220–30.

At the western end of the inner ditch, the later curtain wall of the outer ward stands to an impressive height. The prominent lines of small square holes in the masonry are for the horizontal put-logs which supported timber scaffolding during building and repair work. The plinth of the Mill Tower rests directly on the bare rock. At the base of the stair turret, in the angle of the south curtain wall, is a small trefoiled hood-moulding protecting a sculptured head and shoulders. This a rare survival of the sculpture and decoration which originally adorned the castle.

From here the path leads back to the gatehouse. There is a good view of Beacon Hill across the valley to the south-east. The hill is topped by an earthwork mound which may have been a siegework dating from the years of unrest of King Stephen's reign, or of the minority of Henry III (see p 22).

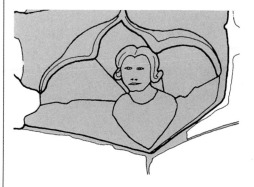

A reconstruction of the sculptured head and shoulders at the junction of the curtain wall and the Mill Tower (drawing: Kate Wilson)

History of the Castle

William the Conqueror directing the building of Hastings Castle, from the Bayeux Tapestry (Michael Holford Library)

The first castle

Pickering stands at a natural crossing point where the east-west route skirting along the northern edge of the valley between marsh and moors meets the north-south route over the moors from Whitby and across the marshes to Malton. There was an important pre-Conquest settlement at Pickering, which was held by Morcar, Earl of Northumbria, at the time of the Norman invasion in 1066. By the time the Domesday Book was compiled (1086), William the Conqueror held Pickering and an extensive district (or Honour) stretching from the River Seven to the west as far as the sea near Filey to the east, and from the marshes of the River Rye to the south across the moors beyond Goathland to the north. To control this wild tract William founded castles at Scarborough and Pickering. Scarborough had already been used as a Roman signal station but Pickering was an unfortified site.

The original earthwork castle at Pickering must date from 1069–70, when William suppressed revolts throughout the North; during this period he built many castles to help him control the English and defend the territory against the Danes and Scots. The motte-and-bailey form was a common design, found in Yorkshire most impressively at York itself and at Tickhill near Doncaster. When Henry I issued a charter at Pickering in 1108 he must have stayed at the earth-and-timber fortification. Throughout the medieval period this strategically important castle remained in royal hands or within the royal family through the earls and dukes of Lancaster.

Across the deep valley of the Pickering Beck is another earthwork castle mound. Beacon Hill, an isolated knoll some 600 yards (550m) west of the castle, may mark the site of a siegework thrown up during the anarchy of Stephen's reign (1135–54) or during the minority of Henry III (1216–20). Such earthworks could be erected rapidly and provided a strategic position for a body of armed men watching a castle garrison with the aim of catching it in an unguarded or weakened moment.

The earthwork on Beacon Hill, to the west of the castle

Owners of Pickering Castle (in red) and kings of England 1066–1413

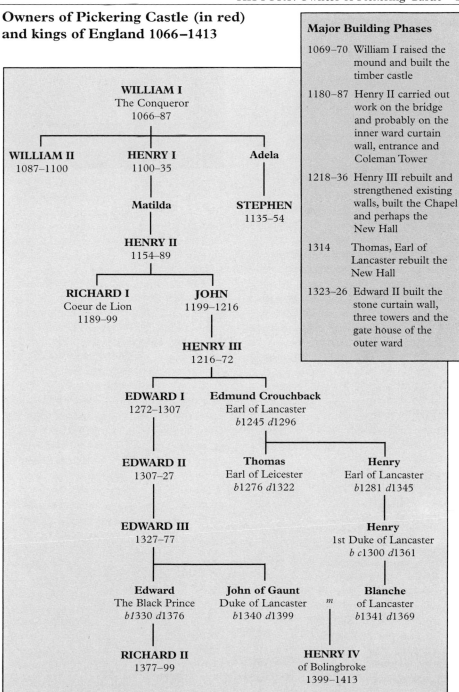

WILLIAM I
The Conqueror
1066–87

WILLIAM II
1087–1100

HENRY I
1100–35

Adela

Matilda

STEPHEN
1135–54

HENRY II
1154–89

RICHARD I
Coeur de Lion
1189–99

JOHN
1199–1216

HENRY III
1216–72

EDWARD I
1272–1307

Edmund Crouchback
Earl of Lancaster
b1245 d1296

EDWARD II
1307–27

Thomas
Earl of Leicester
b1276 d1322

Henry
Earl of Lancaster
b1281 d1345

EDWARD III
1327–77

Henry
1st Duke of Lancaster
b c1300 d1361

Edward
The Black Prince
b1330 d1376

John of Gaunt
Duke of Lancaster
b1340 d1399

m

Blanche
of Lancaster
b1341 d1369

RICHARD II
1377–99

HENRY IV
of Bolingbroke
1399–1413

Major Building Phases

1069–70	William I raised the mound and built the timber castle
1180–87	Henry II carried out work on the bridge and probably on the inner ward curtain wall, entrance and Coleman Tower
1218–36	Henry III rebuilt and strengthened existing walls, built the Chapel and perhaps the New Hall
1314	Thomas, Earl of Lancaster rebuilt the New Hall
1323–26	Edward II built the stone curtain wall, three towers and the gate house of the outer ward

The building of the stone castle

Timber gradually decays and is also vulnerable to destruction by fire. During the twelfth century the majority of the Norman castles were gradually replaced in stone. Architectural evidence suggests that the 'Old Hall' was the first stone building on the site, constructed in the early twelfth century.

Thirteenth-century illustration of a king, his architect and masons (British Library)

There is firmer, documentary evidence from the closing years of the twelfth century in the form of the Pipe Rolls (the annual financial accounts which the sheriffs, as representatives of the king's authority in the shires, rendered to the king). These show a long sequence of replacement and repair at Pickering, starting in the last years of Henry II, continuing through the reigns of his sons Richard I and John, and extending into the first twenty years of the reign of Henry III. Where regular maintenance is involved the sums are small, usually less than £10, but on occasions sums as large as £44 are mentioned. For a modern equivalent all the sums need to be multiplied by at least 120.

The main building work of this period falls into three distinct phases. During the years 1180–87, according to the documentary evidence, there was work on 'the bridge', presumably that at the entrance to the inner ward. It is likely that the curtain wall of the inner ward, the entrance and the Coleman Tower were also built during Henry II's reign. It is possible too that a stone shell keep was placed on the motte at this date, as happened at Tickhill. Henry II had previously built the stone rectangular keep at Scarborough. The second building phase at Pickering was under John, during the years 1207–10. The king visited the castle in 1201 and again in August 1208. The Pipe Rolls mention work on the bridges in 1210, referring to the bridge at

the entrance to the inner ward and either the bridge (i.e. the staircase) approaching the keep or the bridge entering the outer ward.

The third phase is a more extensive one, lasting from 1218 to 1236, and was largely a response to the insecurity and unrest of Henry III's minority (1216–27). The young Henry's position was threatened by both the French, who wanted to claim the throne for the Dauphin Louis, and by a group of rebellious barons in the north of England. The castles of York, Scarborough and Pickering formed a triangle of defence securing the coast and eastern Yorkshire and it seems likely that Pickering Castle was damaged in the civil war that developed as a result of Henry's weak position. Peace was finally established in 1217, and Geoffrey de Nevill, the Sheriff of Yorkshire, was ordered to sustain the castles of Pickering and Scarborough from the revenues of the shire. In 1220 a jury at Pickering enquired 'into what state the castle was in when Geoffrey began work there after the peace, that is how much was then standing, how much fell or was destroyed'.

The main work carried out under Geoffrey was the rebuilding and strengthening of existing walls. The sums involved were considerable. Between 1218

Early in the thirteenth century the wooden keep and walls of the inner ward were replaced in stone; the outer ward palisade remained in wood until the fourteenth century (painting: Ivan Lapper)

and 1226 Geoffrey was estimated to have spent 1000 marks (£667) in the king's service at his two castles, without including direct payments from the king. A further sum of 200 marks (£132) was spent in 1226 when the pace of the work was stepped up. One result of this work was the chapel, first mentioned in 1227. Another may have been a replacement of the outer shell of the keep, judging by the style of its masonry. The New Hall in its earliest form may also date from this period and the entrance would have needed to be brought up to contemporary defensive standards.

By contrast the outer defences remained in timber until the early fourteenth century. During Henry III's reign and beyond, the outer ward or barbican was protected by a palisade of pointed stakes called the herisson; this was maintained by labour services which fell

due every third year. (Although these services are first recorded in 1235 the arrangement is likely to have originated in the eleventh century.) In 1255 each tenant was responsible for one perch (five and a half yards or about 5m) of the herisson; presumably the number of tenants on which this duty fell was sufficient to ensure that the complete length of the herisson bank was kept in good repair. The timber for this work would have come from the adjacent forest. In 1250 ten oaks were cut for repairs on the castle and its mill; in 1251 four oaks were cut and in 1256 forty oaks. As well as for the palisade, these would have been used for floor joists, roof timbers, external half-timbered walling and bridges.

In 1255 the castle was taken out of the care of the sheriff and placed in the custody of the Justiciar, Hugh Bigod. In 1264 war again broke out between Henry

Hugh of Bigod's seal (British Library)

III and his barons, led by Simon de Montfort. After being held captive, Henry was restored to power at Evesham in the following year. Although the war did not seriously affect the northern counties, Bigod supported the king and put the castles at Pickering and Scarborough in a good state of defence. Bigod held Pickering until his death in 1266.

The Lancastrian inheritance

In 1267 the Honour and castle of Pickering were among the lands granted to Henry III's younger son, Edmund Crouchback, as part of the territorial settlement when he was created Earl of Lancaster. (The word 'Honour' refers simply to the area administered by a feudal landlord; at Pickering it was the king or earl.) Edmund held Pickering until his death in 1296. In that year the castle was described as being weak and of no value, its fabric costing £1 to maintain. It was certainly old-fashioned when compared with the compact, multi-towered castles that Edward I and his favoured barons were building in north Wales at that time.

Thomas, Earl of Lancaster (left) facing St George. Thomas's shield bears the Lancastrian coat of arms (Bodleian Library)

Edmund's son, Thomas, Earl of Lancaster, inherited extensive estates and acquired still more by his marriage to the heiress Alice de Lacy. Thomas regarded himself as the leader of the barons against the weak rule of his cousin Edward II. He schemed with the other leading barons against the king's favourite, Piers Gaveston, capturing him at nearby Scarborough Castle in 1312 and executing him after a summary trial. In 1314 Edward was further weakened when he led an English army, which Thomas refused to support, into battle against the Scots at Bannockburn. The result was a humiliating defeat, and in the following years the Scots made repeated raids into the heart of Yorkshire. Finally, in 1321, Thomas declared open rebellion against the king. But Edward rallied support and Thomas was defeated at the Battle of

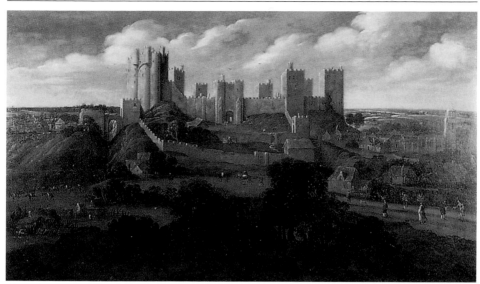

Pontefract Castle: a painting of c1630 (City of Wakefield Metropolitan District Council)

Boroughbridge, imprisoned in his own castle of Pontefract, and executed on a nearby hill in March 1322, an action directly reminiscent of the treatment Thomas had given to Gaveston. The king immediately seized all the Lancastrian lands, including Pickering.

Under Thomas the castle was improved. In 1314 he carried out work on the New Hall to create a fitting residence for the Countess Alice. He also maintained a garrison in the castle and carried out work to improve the defences: 110 oaks were cut for repairs, to renew hourds or brattices ('bretasches') and to supply roof timbers. It is possible that Thomas intended to beautify Pickering as extensively as he had rebuilt Pontefract. However, the events of 1322 came before he could make any major changes.

The fourteenth-century improvements

Following the defeat of Thomas of Lancaster, the king launched another unsuccessful Scottish campaign in the summer of 1322. This provoked Robert Bruce to invade northern England, to burn the town of Ripon and to install his army at Malton; from this position he ravaged the surrounding countryside. Pickering was within easy range of the Scots but the town promised to pay a substantial sum and gave three hostages to support this promise. Pickering Castle and town were thereby saved from attack or pillage. When the Scots withdrew, Edward II appointed a new constable in place of the previous constable who had been taken hostage. The new official, John de Kilvington, was ordered to repair the buildings in the castle, to construct a drawbridge at the entrance to the inner ward and to obtain fresh supplies of munitions. These orders, given verbally in January 1323, were confirmed and extended in August when the king spent three weeks at the castle. In addition to the repairs to existing buildings, rendering of the walls and clearing of existing ditches, the whole herisson stockade was

Edward II's tomb effigy, in Gloucester Cathedral (National Portrait Gallery)

to be replaced by a new stone wall. This work was to include a postern next to the King's Tower (or keep) and a gateway with drawbridge. Another source mentions the provision of towers on this wall. Considerable details survive in the accounts of receipts and expenditure for 1322, 1325 and 1326. These show that extensive use was made of local materials and that the estate of Pickering was expected to finance the building work and still make a profit for the king. It seems likely that Edward II intended to make Pickering a permanent royal possession, well fortified and regularly visited. However, his downfall in December 1326, and his subsequent imprisonment and murder, ended all such plans.

The castle returned to Lancastrian ownership, passing initially to Henry, the younger brother of Earl Thomas, who occasionally stayed at Pickering and held it until his death in 1345. He was

This reconstruction of the fourteenth-century castle shows the stone curtain wall and towers of the outer ward built on the orders of Edward II (painting: Ivan Lapper)

Henry of Bolingbroke, Duke of Lancaster, is proclaimed King Henry IV by the parliament of 1399 (British Library)

succeeded by his warlike son, also called Henry, who was created Duke of Lancaster in 1351. On his death in 1361 the estates passed to Edward III's fourth son, John of Gaunt, through his marriage to Henry's daughter, Blanche. John of Gaunt was created Duke of Lancaster in 1362 when the death of his sister-in-law Maud brought him the entire Lancastrian inheritance. He sometimes visited Pickering and ordered repairs to be carried out, although his major expenditure was on Kenilworth Castle. He died in February 1399.

John of Gaunt's son, Henry of Bolingbroke, had been banished in 1398 by King Richard II (his cousin). This was Henry's punishment for having supported Richard's enemies two years previously. In July 1399, while Richard was in Ireland, Henry landed at Ravenspur, the port at the mouth of the Humber, and came to Pickering to claim his ducal estates. Henry quickly gained support, and, following the forced abdication of Richard II, he claimed the throne as Henry IV. The duchy of Lancaster with all its land was conferred on Henry's son, Henry of Monmouth, but when the young Henry succeeded to the throne as Henry V in 1413 the duchy reverted to the Crown. Ever since that date, although belonging to the Crown, the Duchy of Lancaster estate has always been administered separately from the Crown estate.

Pickering Castle in the later Middle Ages

The duchy records provide an unbroken sequence of accounts from 1399 for the next 300 years. During the fifteenth century they show a regular though small expenditure on maintaining the fabric. In 1441–3 repairs were carried out on the two drawbridges, the roof of the chapel

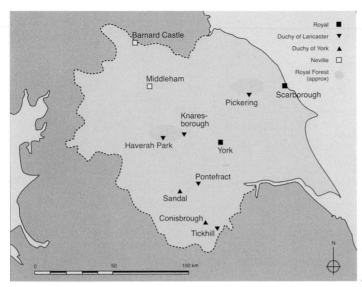

Royal castles of Yorkshire in the fifteenth century

and its chancel, the stables and the Constable's Place and Hall. The stables probably represent the only new building in the fifteenth century; the Constable's Place with its hall may also be a new building or may be an improvement of early timber structures on that site. There is also a reference to a building called 'Le Tresourhouse': this probably refers either to the basement of the Coleman Tower or to the chamber over the Inner Ward entrance. The impression from these records is of a castle in decline, with repairs failing to stem the tide of decay. It could still have been serviceable in the Wars of the Roses but only with considerable outlay on the defences.

The castle under the Tudors and Stuarts

The Tudor monarchs introduced a more cost-effective procedure. Stewards were appointed from the ranks of the local gentry and more regular surveys were introduced. The Cholmleys of nearby Roxby were appointed constables of the castle, stewards of the Honour and foresters of the Forest in 1499, though this became a source of local conflict with the Hastings family, who had previously served in these posts. The first thorough survey was made in 1537, when all the royal castles in the North were surveyed, perhaps in response to the Pilgrimage of Grace, a pro-monastic uprising.

According to this survey, the stables of the outer ward, its curtain wall, the New Hall and the chapel were in good repair; all the rest was in varying states of decay. The drawbridges were in position but had decayed. The curtain wall of the inner ward was in a poor state and a length of 30ft (9m) had fallen down. The towers had retained their timber and lead but all needed extensive repairs, while the keep was 'evil rent, riven and perished', obviously beyond hope of remedy. The surveyor listed the substantial quantities of material (stone, lead, timber, roof-slates), needed to put the castle in order and drew attention to the lack of military weapons: there was not 'any manner of ordnance, artillery or munition of war, nor any place where it could be shot'. Clearly the castle was suitable only for the holding of courts in the Mote Hall and the imprisonment of offenders in the tower basements.

Leland's visit to the castle in about 1535 paints a similar picture:

> The castelle waulles and the toures be meatly [fairly] welle, the logginges yn the ynner court that be of tymbre be in ruine; in this inner court is a chapelle and a cantuarie prest.

There is no mention of where the chantry priest lived. 'The castelle walles now remaining seem to be of no very old building.'

The findings of an Elizabethan jury in about 1565 again provide an account of a castle steadily falling into ruin. This decline had been accelerated by Sir Richard Cholmley, the constable, who had taken the finer stones from the New Hall, thirteen cartloads of stone from the steps of the keep, and two cartloads of

slates to build his new house at Roxby, two miles to the east of the castle. He may also have taken the lead from the Diate Hill Tower. This was not an unusual practice: the constables at Helmsley and Tickhill had built new mansions within the castles in their care.

The next thorough inspection was undertaken by the surveyor John Norden in 1621, soon after the Honour of Pickering has been granted to Charles, Prince of Wales (the future Charles I). His survey shows a further decline in the use of the buildings. The Mote Hall (the New Hall) was ruinous, the tower where the records had been kept was too decayed to use, and all the other towers had some faults in them. Only the Mill Tower was still serviceable as a prison and the chapel was now used as the court-house. The catalogue of repairs needing to be done was lengthening and most of the time the castle was let out on lease.

Engraving of 1823 by Henry Gastineau showing the mound covered in trees. To the right are Rosamund's Tower and the east turret

Pickering Castle played no part in the Civil War (1642–50), unlike its neighbours at Helmsley and Scarborough. It is clear from a survey made in 1651 that the chapel – 'in indifferent good repair' – was the only building still roofed and usable. The damage had been caused by Sir Richard Cholmley and by soldiers stationed in the vicinity during the war. In 1652 the Commonwealth government sold the whole of the duchy estates in Pickering for £6967 8s 7½d, the remains of the castle being valued at £200. At the Restoration, the castle was returned to King Charles II as part of the duchy of Lancaster estates, but its useful life was over.

The chapel was restored in the early nineteenth century. The castle ruins were placed in the care of the Office of Works (now English Heritage) in 1926. The thick growth of trees and bushes which covered the site was gradually cleared and the foundations of many of the courtyard buildings were exposed and consolidated.

Hunting was a popular royal pursuit. This medieval illustration shows King John hunting a stag (British Library)

The Forest and Honour of Pickering

Throughout its active life one of Pickering Castle's main roles was to provide accommodation for the king and his retinue. Most of the kings between 1100 and 1400 visited Pickering, often to enjoy the opportunities for hunting in the surrounding forest. During the reigns of John and Henry III there are records of payments for huntsmen and dogs and for the carriage of carcasses of deer and wild boar to other places, even as far as London. Another favourite pursuit of Pickering's royal owners was horse-rearing. In 1322 Edward II established a stud farm with two stallions, eighteen mares and other younger animals, making a total of about fifty horses.

In this and other ways, the castle and the surrounding terrain (the Honour of Piclcering) were closely interrelated. The area which formed the Honour (also called Pickering Lyth) stretched from the River Seven at Cropton to the coast at Cayton, and from the marshes of the River Rye to the high moors beyond Goathland. The Honour was expected to provide sufficient revenue to maintain and provide for the castle garrison and in addition to make a profit for the Crown. This revenue was to be raised from the resources of the area, which included fish from the rivers, wildfowl from the marshes, crops from the arable fields, cattle from the meadows, deer from the forests and sheep from the moors. Some 1600 sheep are recorded as being kept on the moors within the forest, and the sale of wool was an important source of revenue. The forest was also a source of timber and brushwood, while stone was obtained from the many local quarries.

The Forest of Pickering, which in effect formed the western portion of the Honour, consisted of an area of rough terrain, more scrubland than dense woodland. Its designation as a royal forest

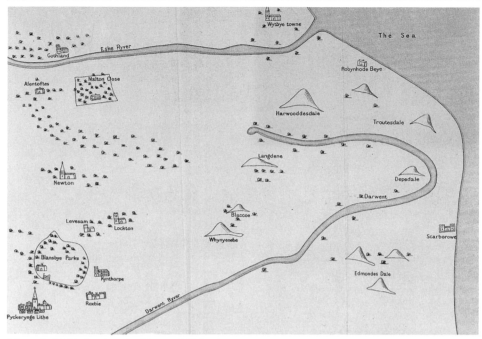

Map of c1650 showing the Forest of Pickering

meant essentially that it was to be maintained as a hunting preserve, reserved exclusively for the use of the king and his officers. Forest Law existed to enforce the royal prerogative over the forest, and gave rise to the castle's other main functions of law court and prison. The law prohibited the killing of red and fallow deer, the collecting of timber, and the clearing of areas of forest for cultivation ('assarting'). The courts imposed heavy fines on those who broke the law (thus adding to the king's revenue), or they sentenced offenders to imprisonment in one of the castle towers. In the fourteenth century the forest deer (some 1300 in all) were even more closely protected within the bounds of Blansby Park, a fenced area to the north of Pickering.

In controlling activity within the Honour of Pickering, the castle and its officials came into close contact with the local community. Indeed the castle officials themselves were often local men. Another point of contact concerned work on the fabric of the castle: local labour would be called upon either for routine maintenance, as in the duties of repairing the herisson and cleaning the mill-ponds, or for new building work.

Tomb of Sir William Bruce, an opponent of Thomas of Lancaster in 1322

Decorated stone capital in Pickering Parish Church

In other respects, Pickering was principally a market town. The straight street of Boroughgate may indicate an element of medieval town planning: here the free burgesses of the town would have lived. This street name is common in many Yorkshire towns, and contrasts with Bondgate, where the bond tenants lived (although no conclusive evidence for a 'Bondgate' has been found in Pickering).

Further evidence of the town's medieval past may be seen in the church of St Peter and St Paul. Norman in origin, the church was altered and extended at various times from the thirteenth to the fifteenth centuries, reflecting the increasing wealth of the town. Two chapels on either side of the chancel were erected by prominent local families, the Bruces and the Roucliffes, both of them connected with the castle. The tomb near the lectern commemorates Sir William Bruce, who fought for the king at the Battle of Boroughbridge when Thomas, Earl of Lancaster was defeated. The tomb in the south chapel is of Sir David and Lady Margary Roucliffe: he was constable of the castle from 1393 to 1407. The fifteenth-century wall paintings in the church are a vivid illustration of the concerns of the townspeople, depicting the miracles of the saints, acts of mercy or human charity, and the dreadful Last Judgement which all mankind would one day have to face.

Further Reading

JONATHAN CLARK, *Helmsley Castle*, 2004

BRIAN K DAVISON, *The New Observer's Book of Castles*, 1986

JOHN GOODALL, *Scarborough Castle*, 2013

JOHN GOODALL, *The English Castle 1066–1650*, 2011

TOM McNEILL, *The English Heritage Book of Castles*, 1992

Glossary

ashlar dressings masonry of large blocks dressed to even faces and square edges

barbican an outwork protecting a gateway, or an outer court which protects an inner courtyard

bond tenant a tenant who was bound to provide a labour service as a part of his tenure; later changed to a money payment

brattice a timber covering, usually an additional defence to a wall-top (see 'hourd'), but sometimes brushwood laid to protect building work during the winter when it was unwise to lay mortared stonework

chamfer a surface made by cutting across the square angle of a stone block, usually at an angle of 45 degrees to the other two surfaces

chantry chapel a chapel endowed for the saying of masses for the souls of the founders and their families

corbel a projection from a wall, intended to support the weight of a wall or parapet above it

cornice a projecting decorative feature along the top of a wall or arch

cruciform in the form of a cross

cusp a projecting point forming a leaf shape in the tracery of a Gothic door-arch or window-head

dripstone a projecting moulding above an arch or lintel to throw off surface water

fluting vertical channelling in the shaft of a column or a door arch

herisson a barrier of pointed wooden stakes, arranged randomly in the ground to prevent a direct approach by attackers; the name comes from the French word for hedgehog, which these stakes resembled

hourd covered wooden gallery attached to the top of the external wall of a stone castle for defence of the base of the wall. They were supported on wooden brackets, the horizontal holes for which are sometimes visible

jamb shaft stones forming the straight side of an archway, doorway or window

lancet window a narrow window with a pointed head

motte a castle mound, usually of earth or turf; the strongpoint of an earthwork-and-timber castle

newel staircase a winding spiral staircase, either set in the thickness of a wall or in a separate turret

plinth horizontal course(s) of finer stones at the base of a wall to provide a better foundation, often projecting from the vertical wall-face and chamfered on top

postern a back door, often in a concealed position

put-log a short horizontal timber used in scaffolding for building or repair work; put-log holes are often left unfilled after construction has been completed

quoins large stones set at the vertical angles of a building, usually of finer or stronger stone than the rest of the walling

shell keep a great tower with a continuous outer wall, usually circular, against which subsidiary domestic buildings are placed

slit a narrow opening in a wall for admitting light and for discharging arrows

splayed opening a window- or door-opening with angled sides between the actual opening and the wall-face, permitting more light to enter than is possible with straight sides

string-course continuous horizontal moulding on the external face of a wall, often defining internal floor levels

transomed a horizontally divided window

ward a courtyard or bailey

The martyrdom of St Edmund: one of several fifteenth-century wall paintings in Pickering Parish Church